THIS BOOK BELONGS TO

_____

FOR THE KIDS WHO WANT
SPECIAL CHRISTMAS PRESENT

ISBN: 9798894581897

HENRY PRESSED HIS NOSE AGAINST THE FROSTY WINDOW. SNOWFLAKES
DANCED IN THE MOONLIGHT, PAINTING THE WORLD WHITE.
"I WISH I COULD HELP SANTA," HE WHISPERED.

AT THE NORTH POLE, SANTA AND HIS ELVES BUSTLED ABOUT, PREPARING FOR CHRISTMAS. LAUGHTER AND THE SOUND OF JINGLING BELLS FILLED THE AIR AS TOYS WERE LOADED INTO THE SLEIGH.

SUDDENLY, THE WORKSHOP DOORS BURST OPEN. A CHILLING WIND SWEPT INSIDE, EXTINGUISHING THE WARM GLOW OF THE CANDLES. SHADOWS STRETCHED ACROSS THE WALLS AS ICY FOG FILLED THE ROOM.

FROM THE FOG EMERGED FROSTVEIL, AN ANCIENT GHOST WITH GLIMMERING FROST ROBES AND ICY BLUE EYES. "YOUR TIME SPREADING JOY IS OVER, SANTA!" FROSTVEIL'S VOICE ECHOED, COLD AS THE ARCTIC.

SANTA REACHED FOR HIS MAGIC STAFF, BUT FROSTVEIL WAS FASTER. WITH A SWIRL OF ICY MAGIC, HE TRAPPED SANTA IN A SHIMMERING ICE PRISON. "NOW, CHRISTMAS WILL FREEZE FOREVER!"

THE ELVES TRIED TO FIGHT BACK, BUT FROSTVEIL'S POWER WAS TOO STRONG. SANTA'S REINDEER FLED INTO THE SNOWY WILDERNESS, SEEKING SOMEONE BRAVE ENOUGH TO SAVE HIM AND CHRISTMAS.

IN A SMALL TOWN FAR AWAY, HENRY HEARD A SOFT THUMP OUTSIDE. CURIOUS, HE PEEKED OUT AND GASPED. ONE OF SANTA'S REINDEER, DASHER, STOOD TREMBLING IN THE SNOW.

HENRY RAN OUTSIDE, WRAPPING DASHER IN A WARM BLANKET. "WHAT'S WRONG, BUDDY?" HE ASKED. DASHER'S EYES GLOWED AS HE SHOWED HENRY A VISION OF SANTA TRAPPED IN FROSTVEIL'S ICY LAIR.

HENRY'S HEART RACED. "SANTA'S IN TROUBLE?" DASHER NODDED, PAWING THE GROUND URGENTLY. "THEN I'LL HELP! WE HAVE TO SAVE CHRISTMAS!" HENRY GRABBED HIS COAT AND SCARF, READY FOR THE ADVENTURE.

DASHER KNELT, LETTING HENRY CLIMB ONTO HIS BACK. TOGETHER, THEY TOOK OFF
INTO THE FROSTY NIGHT SKY, HEADING TOWARD FROSTVEIL'S ICY
LAIR DEEP IN THE MOUNTAINS.

THE WIND HOWLED AS DASHER FLEW OVER SNOWY FORESTS AND ICY RIVERS.
HENRY HELD TIGHT, HIS SCARF FLUTTERING BEHIND HIM. "WE'LL SAVE SANTA,"
HE WHISPERED, BRAVING THE BITTER COLD.

DASHER LANDED IN A DARK FOREST WHERE THE TREES LOOMED LIKE SHADOWY GIANTS. THE AIR WAS EERILY SILENT, EXCEPT FOR THE CRUNCH OF SNOW UNDERFOOT.

HENRY SPOTTED GLOWING FOOTPRINTS LEADING DEEPER INTO THE WOODS.
"FROSTVEIL'S TRAIL," HE SAID. GATHERING HIS COURAGE, HE FOLLOWED THE LIGHT,
EVERY STEP BRINGING HIM CLOSER TO DANGER.

THE TREES WHISPERED WARNINGS IN THE WIND. "TURN BACK, LITTLE ONE,"
THE VOICES SEEMED TO SAY. HENRY SHOOK HIS HEAD. "I CAN'T. SANTA NEEDS ME."

THE FOREST GREW DARKER. SUDDENLY, A SHIMMERING FROST WOLF EMERGED, BLOCKING HENRY'S PATH. ITS EYES GLOWED AN ICY BLUE, AND ITS GROWL SENT CHILLS DOWN HENRY'S SPINE.

THE WOLF LUNGED, BUT DASHER CHARGED TO PROTECT HENRY. WITH A POWERFUL KICK, DASHER SHATTERED THE ICY CREATURE INTO SPARKLING SHARDS. "THANKS, DASHER," HENRY SAID, CATCHING HIS BREATH.

THE GLOWING TRAIL LED TO A FROZEN RIVER. THE ICE CRACKED UNDER
HENRY'S FEET AS HE CAREFULLY CROSSED. "DON'T LOOK DOWN,"
HE MUTTERED, CLUTCHING DASHER'S REINS.

ON THE OTHER SIDE, THE TRAIL VANISHED INTO A WALL OF ICY MIST.
HENRY HESITATED. "WE'RE CLOSE," HE SAID, STEPPING FORWARD,
THE MIST CHILLING HIM TO THE BONE.

THROUGH THE MIST, HENRY SAW FROSTVEIL'S LAIR—A TOWERING
ICE CASTLE WITH GLOWING BLUE SPIRES. THE WIND HOWLED LOUDER,
WARNING HIM TO STAY AWAY. "WE HAVE TO DO THIS," HENRY SAID.

DASHER PAWED AT THE ICE AS HENRY APPROACHED THE MASSIVE DOORS. HE TOOK A DEEP BREATH AND PUSHED THEM OPEN. THE SOUND ECHOED THROUGH THE FROZEN HALLS.

INSIDE THE ICE CASTLE, FROST-COVERED CHANDELIERS HUNG FROM THE CEILING.
HENRY'S BREATH FOGGED IN THE COLD AIR AS HE STEPPED CAREFULLY,
HIS BOOTS CRUNCHING ON THE ICY FLOOR.

THE FIRST HALLWAY WAS LINED WITH MIRRORS. EACH MIRROR SHOWED DISTORTED, ICY VERSIONS OF HENRY. "A TRICK," HE SAID ALOUD. BUT WHICH PATH WAS REAL?

HENRY TOSSED A PEBBLE ONTO THE MIRRORED PATHS. ONE MIRROR SHATTERED, REVEALING A HIDDEN DROP BELOW. "NICE TRY, FROSTVEIL," HENRY SAID, CHOOSING THE SAFE PATH.

THE NEXT ROOM WAS FILLED WITH GLITTERING ICE CROCODILES. THEY LAY STILL, BLENDING WITH THE ICY GROUND. "ARE THEY ALIVE?" HENRY WHISPERED TO DASHER.

THE MOMENT HENRY STEPPED FORWARD, THE CROCODILES CAME TO LIFE,
SNAPPING THEIR ICY JAWS. DASHER LEAPED, DODGING
A SNAPPING CROCODILE JUST IN TIME.

HENRY SPOTTED A LEVER ON THE FAR WALL. "IF I PULL THAT, MAYBE I
CAN STOP THEM!" HE DARTED THROUGH THE CROCODILES, HIS HEART RACING.

ONE CROCODILE LUNGED, BUT DASHER KICKED IT ASIDE. HENRY REACHED THE LEVER AND YANKED IT. THE CROCODILES FROZE BACK INTO STATUES. "THAT WAS CLOSE!"

BEYOND THE CROCODILES, A STAIRCASE SPIRALED UPWARD. HENRY CLIMBED CAUTIOUSLY, GRIPPING THE ICY RAILING. THE AIR GREW COLDER WITH EACH STEP, FROST FORMING ON HIS SCARF.

AT THE TOP, HENRY ENTERED A ROOM FILLED WITH SLITHERING FROST SNAKES. THEIR EYES GLOWED BLUE, AND THEIR HISS SOUNDED LIKE THE HOWLING WIND.

HENRY SAW A FROZEN TORCH ON THE WALL. "IF I CAN LIGHT THAT, MAYBE IT'LL
SCARE THE SNAKES AWAY!" HE GRABBED DASHER'S REINS AND
EDGED TOWARD THE TORCH.

ONE SNAKE LUNGED, ITS ICY FANGS MISSING HENRY BY INCHES. "STAY CALM,"
HE TOLD HIMSELF, USING A FLINT FROM HIS POCKET TO STRIKE A SPARK.

THE SPARK IGNITED THE TORCH, AND A WARM ORANGE GLOW SPREAD THROUGH THE ROOM. THE SNAKES RECOILED, SLITHERING BACK INTO THE SHADOWS. "THAT DID IT!" HENRY CHEERED.

HENRY AND DASHER HURRIED THROUGH THE DOOR, FINDING THEMSELVES IN A
GRAND HALL. A MASSIVE ICY CHANDELIER DANGLED ABOVE,
AND FROSTVEIL'S LAUGH ECHOED.

"YOU'RE BRAVER THAN I THOUGHT, LITTLE ONE," FROSTVEIL'S VOICE BOOMED.
"BUT YOU'LL NEVER SAVE SANTA!"

THE FLOOR SHIFTED BENEATH THEM, REVEALING A DEEP PIT FILLED WITH FREEZING WATER. HENRY GRABBED DASHER, JUST BARELY AVOIDING THE TRAP.

"YOU'LL NEED MORE THAN LUCK," FROSTVEIL SNEERED, HIS ICY FORM APPEARING IN A SWIRL OF FROST. HIS COLD EYES GLARED DOWN AT HENRY.

Christmas magic **is stronger** than your icy tricks!

HENRY STOOD TALL, HIS BREATH VISIBLE IN THE ICY AIR. "YOU CAN'T WIN, FROSTVEIL. CHRISTMAS MAGIC IS STRONGER THAN YOUR ICY TRICKS!"

FROSTVEIL WAVED HIS HAND, SUMMONING SHARDS OF ICE THAT FLEW
TOWARD HENRY AND DASHER. "LET'S SEE HOW STRONG YOU ARE!"

HENRY DUCKED BEHIND A FALLEN COLUMN AS THE SHARDS SHATTERED
AROUND HIM. HE SPOTTED A GLOWING CRYSTAL EMBEDDED IN THE CEILING.
"THAT MUST BE HIS POWER SOURCE!"

"DASHER, WE NEED TO HIT THAT CRYSTAL!" HENRY SAID. DASHER NODDED,
READY TO CHARGE AS HENRY LOOKED FOR A WAY TO AIM AT THE CEILING.

THE ICY AIR GREW COLDER AS HENRY AND DASHER VENTURED DEEPER INTO FROSTVEIL'S LAIR. FROST-COVERED STATUES OF STRANGE CREATURES LINED THE WALLS, THEIR HOLLOW EYES WATCHING.

AS HENRY STEPPED FORWARD, THE STATUES CAME ALIVE. ICE GARGOYLES LEAPED FROM THEIR PEDESTALS, THEIR CLAWS SHARP AND GLINTING.

"RUN, DASHER!" HENRY SHOUTED, WEAVING THROUGH THE SNARLING CREATURES. ONE GARGOYLE LUNGED, BUT DASHER KICKED IT ASIDE, CRACKING ITS ICY BODY.

HENRY SPOTTED A GLOWING RUNE ON THE WALL. "THAT MUST CONTROL THEM!"
HE SPRINTED TOWARD IT, DODGING CLAWS AND ICY SHARDS FLYING THROUGH THE AIR.

REACHING THE RUNE, HENRY PRESSED HIS HAND AGAINST IT. WARMTH SURGED THROUGH HIS FINGERS, AND THE GARGOYLES FROZE MID-ATTACK, CRUMBLING BACK INTO STATUES.

THEY MOVED INTO THE NEXT CHAMBER, WHERE A RIVER OF FREEZING
WATER FLOWED. THIN, JAGGED ICE BRIDGES STRETCHED ACROSS IT, CREAKING OMINOUSLY.

HENRY TESTED THE FIRST BRIDGE, HIS HEART POUNDING. IT CRACKED
BUT HELD. SLOWLY, HE AND DASHER MOVED ACROSS, ONE CAREFUL STEP AT A TIME.

HALFWAY ACROSS, THE ICE SHATTERED. HENRY GRABBED THE EDGE,
PULLING HIMSELF UP WITH SHAKING ARMS. DASHER LEAPED TO SAFETY,
HIS HOOVES SKIDDING ON THE FAR SIDE.

IN THE NEXT ROOM, FROSTVEIL'S LAUGHTER ECHOED. "YOU'RE PERSISTENT, BOY, BUT YOU'LL NEVER REACH SANTA!" THE WALLS CLOSED IN, SPIKES OF ICE JUTTING TOWARD HENRY.

HENRY SPOTTED A LEVER. "AGAIN WITH THE LEVERS!" HE MUTTERED,
RUNNING TOWARD IT AS THE SPIKED WALLS CREPT CLOSER.
HE YANKED IT, STOPPING THE WALLS JUST IN TIME.

THE ROOM SHIFTED, REVEALING A MAZE OF ICY CORRIDORS. "STAY CLOSE, DASHER," HENRY SAID, HIS BREATH FOGGING THE AIR. "THIS PLACE IS A TRAP."

THE MAZE TWISTED AND TURNED, THE ICY WALLS REFLECTING THEIR FACES. SOME PATHS WERE BLOCKED BY SHARP ICICLES, OTHERS LED TO DEAD ENDS.

SUDDENLY, AN ICY SERPENT SLITHERED INTO THEIR PATH, ITS GLOWING
BLUE EYES FIXED ON HENRY. IT HISSED, ITS FROZEN FANGS DRIPPING WITH FROST.

HENRY SWUNG HIS TORCH, KEEPING THE SERPENT AT BAY. DASHER CHARGED, DISTRACTING IT AS HENRY FOUND AN OPENING IN THE WALL.

THE SERPENT LUNGED, BUT HENRY ROLLED ASIDE AND SHOVED A SHARD OF GLOWING ICE INTO ITS MOUTH. THE SERPENT SHATTERED INTO ICY DUST.

THEY ENTERED THE FINAL CHAMBER, WHERE FROSTVEIL'S THRONE STOOD
ATOP A JAGGED ICE PLATFORM. SANTA REMAINED TRAPPED IN
A TOWERING BLOCK OF ICE.

FROSTVEIL APPEARED, HIS ICY FORM SHIMMERING. "YOU'VE COME FAR, BOY, BUT THIS IS WHERE YOUR JOURNEY ENDS!" HE BELLOWED, RAISING HIS FROSTY HANDS.

SHARDS OF ICE RAINED DOWN FROM THE CEILING. HENRY DODGED,
SHIELDING DASHER. HE NOTICED A GLOWING CRYSTAL ABOVE FROSTVEIL'S THRONE.
"THAT MUST BE HIS POWER SOURCE!"

DASHER CHARGED, DRAWING FROSTVEIL'S ATTENTION. HENRY CLIMBED THE ICY PLATFORM, GRIPPING THE JAGGED EDGES AS FROSTVEIL'S ICY MAGIC SWIRLED AROUND HIM.

FROSTVEIL SPOTTED HENRY AND UNLEASHED A FREEZING BLAST. HENRY DUCKED BEHIND THE THRONE, HIS FINGERS BRUSHING THE GLOWING CRYSTAL EMBEDDED IN THE ICE.

HENRY PULLED OUT HIS SLINGSHOT, LOADING A SHARP SHARD OF ICE.
"THIS IS FOR CHRISTMAS!" HE SHOUTED, AIMING FOR THE GLOWING CRYSTAL.

THE SHARD STRUCK TRUE, CRACKING THE CRYSTAL. FROSTVEIL STAGGERED,
HIS ICY FORM FLICKERING. "NO! YOU CANNOT DEFEAT ME!"

HENRY CLIMBED HIGHER AND STRUCK THE CRYSTAL WITH ALL HIS STRENGTH.
IT SHATTERED INTO A MILLION PIECES, AND FROSTVEIL LET OUT A PIERCING SCREAM.

THE ICY LAIR BEGAN TO MELT. FROSTVEIL'S FORM DISSOLVED INTO MIST, HIS VOICE FADING. "THIS ISN'T OVER..."

SANTA'S ICE PRISON CRACKED, AND THE WARMTH OF CHRISTMAS MAGIC
FILLED THE ROOM. HENRY AND DASHER RUSHED TO HIS SIDE.

"HENRY, YOU SAVED CHRISTMAS!" SANTA SAID, STEPPING OUT OF THE BROKEN ICE PRISON. "YOU'VE SHOWN INCREDIBLE COURAGE AND HEART."

DASHER NUZZLED HENRY AS SANTA'S SLEIGH APPEARED, THE BAG OF PRESENTS
GLOWING WITH MAGIC. "LET'S FINISH DELIVERING THESE GIFTS!"
SANTA SAID WITH A SMILE.

THE SLEIGH SOARED INTO THE NIGHT SKY, THE STARS TWINKLING ABOVE.
HENRY LOOKED DOWN AT THE SNOWY TOWNS BELOW, FILLED
WITH CHRISTMAS CHEER.

BACK AT THE NORTH POLE, THE ELVES CHEERED FOR HENRY AND DASHER. SANTA HANDED HENRY A SPECIAL BELL. "A TOKEN OF YOUR BRAVERY," HE SAID.

AS HENRY RANG THE BELL, HE FELT THE TRUE MAGIC OF CHRISTMAS IN HIS HEART.
THE SLEIGH DISAPPEARED INTO THE STARS AS SANTA'S VOICE ECHOED,
"MERRY CHRISTMAS TO ALL, AND TO ALL A GOOD NIGHT!"

www.ingramcontent.com/pod-product-compliance
Lightning Source LLC
Chambersburg PA
CBHW081539120626

46550CB00009B/2791

* 9 7 9 8 8 8 9 4 5 8 1 8 9 7 *